D uring the 1960s the Royal National lifeboat Institution (RNLI) began to introduce faster all-weather lifeboats, starting with a 44ft steel-hulled self-righting type, which was purchased from the United States Coast Guard in 1963 and taken on trials around Britain. The acquisition of this boat was a significant step forward for the RNLI, as the design was radically different from British lifeboats built in the immediate post-war era in many ways. The 44-footer, numbered 44-001 and self-righting by virtue of its watertight cabins, was faster – at about fifteen knots – than conventional displacement-hulled lifeboats then in service, more powerful and offered better crew and casualty protection.

The new type, designated Waveney after the river where the first of the RNLI boats were built, went on to be a highly successful design and the twenty-two boats of the class that were built for service in the UK and Ireland were well-liked at those stations which operated them. The

▼ The first 44ft Waveney built in Britain, John F. Kennedy (ON.1001), operational number 44-002, pictured during builder's trials off Lowestoft in 1966.

A NELSON FOR THE NETHERLANDS • The Keith Nelson design proved to be well suited for work in heavy weather, and so in 1966 the South Holland Lifeboat Society, the KNZHRM, purchased one for service off the coast of the Netherlands. The KNZHRM was looking for faster lifeboats to undertake rescues in reasonably calm weather and at greater distances from the coast. To avoid high development costs, the proven 40ft Nelson was considered and one was ordered. The boat, named Komer in KNZHRM service, was capable of twenty-eight knots, with power coming from two 375hp Caterpillar D336TA engines, and had a range at full speed of 250 miles. She measured 12.52m by 3.66m, and, after evaluation trials, served at Terschelling, on the country's north coast, from 1972 to 1979, operating alongside the conventional motor lifeboat Carlot. She was sold out of service in 1980.

Waveney proved that cutting-edge technology could be beneficial, that fast lifeboats' sea-keeping qualities were more than good enough for search and rescue work, and that greater speed was a significant bonus when demands on the lifeboat service were increasing as a result of more people using the sea for leisure purposes and, as a result, services were often being undertaken in benign weather.

Following the successful introduction of the Waveney, RNLI staff began to look at faster lifeboats in the late 1960s, as speed was becoming a significant factor in rescue work. The faster the lifeboat, the faster a casualty could be reached, thus reducing the chances of a situation deteriorating and making a rescue more difficult. A 52ft all-weather lifeboat, the Arun class, was developed, and at the same time a smaller

Lifeboat Design and Development No.6

BREDE
CLASS LIFEBOATS

The RNLI's Brede class intermediate lifeboats, their design and history

Nicholas Leach
FOXGLOVE PUBLISHING

First published 2021

Published by
Foxglove Publishing Ltd
Foxglove House, Shute Hill,
Lichfield WS13 8DB
United Kingdom
Tel 07940 905046

ISBN 9781909540217

Typesetting/layout by
Nicholas Leach/
Foxglove Publishing

THE LIFEBOAT DESIGN AND DEVELOPMENT SERIES

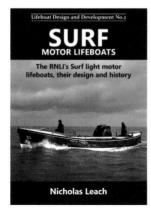

Lifeboat Design and Development No.2

SURF
MOTOR LIFEBOATS
The RNLI's Surf light motor
lifeboats, their design and history

Nicholas Leach

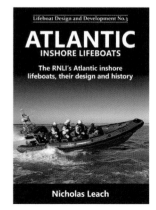

Lifeboat Design and Development No.3

ATLANTIC
INSHORE LIFEBOATS
The RNLI's Atlantic inshore
lifeboats, their design and history

Nicholas Leach

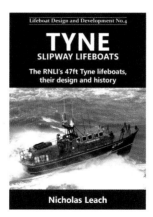

Lifeboat Design and Development No.4

TYNE
SLIPWAY LIFEBOATS
The RNLI's 47ft Tyne lifeboats,
their design and history

Nicholas Leach

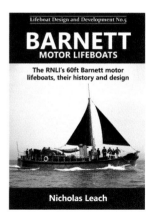

Lifeboat Design and Development No.5

BARNETT
MOTOR LIFEBOATS
The RNLI's 60ft Barnett motor
lifeboats, their history and design

Nicholas Leach

LIFEBOAT DESIGN AND DEVELOPMENT SERIES This is the sixth in a series of concise illustratved volumes that trace the history of and describe technical aspects of RNLI motor lifeboat types. The first volume in the series covered the Clyde class rescue cruisers, and the other volumes encompass the small Surf motor lifeboats, Atlantic inshore lifeboats and the 47ft Tyne fast slipway lifeboats.

THE AUTHOR Nicholas Leach has a long-standing interest in lifeboats and the lifeboat service. He has written many articles, books and papers on the subject, including a history of the origins of the lifeboat service; a comprehensive record of the RNLI's lifeboat stations in 1999, the organisation's 175th anniversary; RNLI Motor Lifeboats, a detailed history of the development of powered lifeboats; and numerous station histories, including ones covering the stations of Cromer, Longhope, Padstow, Sennen Cove, Weymouth and Humber. He has visited all of the lifeboat stations in the UK and Ireland, past and present, and is Editor of Ships Monthly, the international shipping magazine, and Lifeboats Past & Present, the magazine for lifeboat enthusiasts.

Contents

Acknowledgements

A number of people have assisted with this small publication, which records the history and development of the Brede class lifeboats. I am very grateful to the following for assisting in various ways: Michael Vlasto, former RNLI Operations Director, for sharing his experience of Brede class lifeboats; Hayley Whiting and the RNLI Heritage team for continuing to facilitate my research; Eleanor Driscoll, at the RNLI, for assisting with the supply of images; Mark Hughes, Director Capital Projects, National Sea Rescue Institute, South Africa; Leonie Mead, Oban Lifeboat Press Officer; and Ian Moignard, who thoroughly proofed the text, providing comments to greatly improve the content. *Nicholas Leach, Lichfield, May 2021*

Bibliography

Anon (1980): The Brede: prototype of a new experimental lifeboat based on the Lochin 33 (Lifeboat, Vol.XLVII, no.472, Summer, pp.48-50).

Leach, Nicholas (2019): Powering to the Rescue (Lily Publications, Isle of Man).

Over, Lt Cdr H.E. (RNLI Chief Technical Officer) (1983): Brede Class lifeboat development a commercial design as a fast lifeboat (Lifeboat International, 1983 edition, pp.18-26).

Pike, Dag (1980): New trend in developing workboat hull designs (Lloyds List 23.7.1980).

Summary of the 33ft Brede lifeboats

ON Op No	Year / Yard no Builder	Name Donor	Cost Displcmt*	Stations
1066 33-01	1979 (1066) Lochin Marine	**[Not named]** RNLI General Funds.	£107,628 –	Trials only 1980-82
1080 33-02	1982 (1080) Lochin Marine	**Ann Ritchie** Gift of Mrs A. A. Ritchie, Isle of Man.	£157,169 9.45 tonnes	Oban 25.10.1982- 19.9.1987
1083 33-03	1982 (1083) Lochin Marine	**Leonore Chilcott** Gift of Mr Paul Chilcott, Guernsey.	£153,475 8.64 tonnes	Fowey 16.10.1982- 1.1988
1083 33-04	1982 (1084) Lochin Marine	**Philip Vaux** Bequest of Mrs Elizabeth Felicity Vaux.	£155,939 8.64 tonnes	Girvan 16.2.1983-4.1989
1087 33-05	1983 (1087) Lochin Marine	**Merchant Navy** Merchant Navy Appeal.	£152,207 8.64 tonnes	Relief 18.4.1983-9.1987 Oban 19.9.1987-3.1989
1088 33-06	1983 (1088) Lochin Marine	**Caroline Finch** Legacies of Mr W.H. Finch, Mr H.E. Rohll, Mrs M.G. Shaw and Mr W. J. Orley.	£155,645 8.74 tonnes	Exmouth 4.8.1983- 8.7.1994
1089 33-07	1983 (1089) Lochin Marine	**Inner Wheel** Inner Wheel Clubs of GB and Ireland.	£154,043 8.69 tonnes	Poole 10.1983-9.2001 Calshot 12.2001-4.2002
1090 33-08	1984 (1090) Lochin Marine	**Foresters Future** Ancient Order of Foresters, plus other gifts and legacies.	£160,984 8.79 tonnes	Alderney 10.3.1984- 1986 Relief 10.1986-2.9.2002
1101 33-09	1984 (1101) Lochin Marine	**Enid of Yorkshire** Gift of Arnold T. Sanderson, North Ferriby, North Humberside.	£177,331 9.45 tonnes	Relief 22.6.1984- 8.9.1997
1102 33-10	1984 (1102) Lochin Marine	**Nottinghamshire** The Nottinghamshire Lifeboat Appeal.	£179,079 8.69 tonnes	Invergordon 16.7.1984- 7.1988 Oban 26.3.1989-7.1997
1104 33-11	1985 (1104) Lochin Marine	**Safeway** Safeway Food Stores Appeal.	£184,775 8.69 tonnes	Calshot 24.3.1985- 12.2001
1105 33-12	1985 (1105) Lochin Marine	**Amateur Swimming Associations** Amateur Swimming Associations of England, Scotland and Wales.	£186,421 8.69 tonnes	Relief 30.5.1985-1989 Girvan 11.4.1989- 29.8.1993

* Displacement The measurement is in metric tonnes, with one ton equivalent to 1,000kg

Introduction

Brede class intermediate lifeboats were introduced into the RNLI fleet in the 1980s, and they were an unusual departure for the life-saving charity in terms of boat design and development. During the 1970s the RNLI explored the possibilities of introducing new lifeboats of about 35ft overall. The intention was that boats of this size should be available for allocation to stations whose operational requirements demanded a lifeboat larger, and with greater range, than the Atlantic 21 rigid inflatable, an inshore lifeboat, but where a boat with the longer endurance of the 37ft 6in Rother, then the smallest of the Institution's modern displacement lifeboats, would not be justified.

A design of boat which was fast, essentially simple to build and maintain, but which had outstanding seakeeping qualities, was

▼ Relief Brede class Foresters Future (33-08) at Calshot. (By courtesy of the RNLI)

required. The boat deemed to meet these requirements was the Lochin 33, a commercial design initiated at Rye on the Sussex coast, and which the RNLI developed into the Brede class lifeboat. The Bredes, according to former RNLI Director Michael Vlasto, were a 'big little boat', and despite their size they proved to be fine life-saving craft and were well-liked at the stations where they served. The Lochin design benefited from outstanding sea-keeping characteristics, provided good manoeuvrability and speed, and gave good crew protection. This book provides a history of the design and describes the individual boats, many of which went on to have fine life-saving careers in South Africa.

commercial hull design was assessed, in the shape of a 40ft Keith Nelson boat. The Keith Nelson design was based on a semi-displacement hull form, which was first built in 1958, when Peter Thornycroft, whose grandfather Sir John Thornycroft had founded the famous boatbuilding firm of John I. Thornycroft and Co on the Thames, saw that a wooden 23ft launch proved surprisingly fast thanks to its unusual hull form. Thornycroft developed the hull, giving it a deep and sharp entry for a soft ride in head seas, and in 1962 the GRP-hulled Nelson 34 was built.

The Royal Navy bought many Keith Nelsons, including two VIP launches for the Royal Yacht Britannia. The 34ft boat was followed by a 40ft version, with Trinity House using the latter as a pilot cutter, which proved ideal for safely taking pilots out to ships in any weather. As the Keith Nelson design proved to be well suited for work in heavy weather, in 1966 the South Holland Lifeboat Society, the KNZHRM, decided to purchase one for service off the coast of the Netherlands and, after evaluation, it gave eight years of service. The RNLI also looked at the Keith Nelson in the late 1960s, and acquired a Nelson 40 in 1968.

This boat, official number (ON) 1017, was constructed in glass reinforced plastic (GRP), being the first RNLI lifeboat built of this material, and it can be regarded as the forerunner of the intermediate lifeboat, for which speed was a major consideration. Designed by TT Boat Designs Ltd, of Bembridge, IOW, with a hull moulded by Halmatic at Havant,

◀ The Atlantic 21 rigid inflatable inshore lifeboat B-541 Elizabeth Bestwick. (By courtesy of the RNLI)

▲ The RNLI's sole Keith Nelson lifeboat, Ernest William and Elizabeth Ellen Hinde (ON.1017), heading out of Sheerness Docks on trials on 5 June 1969. (Jeff Morris, by courtesy of the RNLI) ▶

ON.1017 was used to test whether a standard GRP hull could withstand severe weather conditions and enable the RNLI to assess the material's suitability for future lifeboat construction. The intention was to find a lifeboat as seaworthy as conventional lifeboats but faster and, by using GRP in the construction, built at substantially lower cost at a time when wooden boatbuilding was becoming ever more expensive.

Fitted with twin Thornycroft six-cylinder four-stroke turbo-charged diesel engines developing 125hp at 2,400rpm, the boat had a maximum speed of nineteen knots and a cruising speed of seventeen. With a fuel capacity of 320 gallons, she had a range of 440 nautical miles at her cruising speed. The boat, operational number 40-001, was the only Keith Nelson operated by the RNLI. ON.1017 underwent lengthy sea trials following her introduction in 1969, before being sent to selected stations for operational evaluation. As part of her trials, she was sent for evaluation to Sheerness, on the River Medway, guarding the southern shores of the Thames Estuary, with a view to Sheerness becoming a new lifeboat station.

She remained at Sheerness from April to November 1969, proving the need for all-weather lifeboat cover in the area, and then went to Calshot, where she established another new station at the mouth of the Solent, and was named Ernest William and Elizabeth Ellen Hinde. Although ON.1017 proved that GRP was a suitable material for lifeboat design, a major drawback of the Keith Nelson design was that it was not self-righting. So, by the mid-1980s, with the RNLI aiming to operate a fleet entirely of self-righting lifeboats, it was taken out of service as soon as a suitable replacement – the 33ft Brede – was available.

During the 1970s the RNLI continued to experiment with various different designs of both all-weather and inshore lifeboats. Inshore lifeboats (ILBs), in the form of a 16ft inflatable with a single outboard

◄ The Keith Nelson lifeboat Ernest William and Elizabeth Ellen Hinde (ON.1017), served at Calshot for fifteen years. Provided from the legacy of Mrs E.E. Hinde, of Darlington, she is pictured at her naming ceremony at Calshot on 28 July 1972. (By courtesy of the RNLI)

engine, had been introduced in the early 1960s and proved to be outstandingly effective rescue craft, with the numbers in service gradually increasing during the decade. To supplement the 16ft inflatable, larger and more capable ILBs were also developed, including rigid hulled craft, such as the 18ft 6in McLachlan, and larger twin-engined inflatables with rigid hulls, the Atlantic 21. The Atlantic has since been further developed and improved, and has become one of the most successful designs of lifeboat ever. Since its development at Atlantic College, in South Wales, in the late 1960s, more Atlantics have been built for service with the RNLI than any other lifeboat type.

The idea behind its development was to improve on the basic inflatable ILB. A boat with greater speed, crew comfort and general capabilities was needed, and fitting sponsons to a rigid hull provided an excellent rescue boat, and the concept proved so successful that during the 1970s the RNLI designed a larger rigid inflatable. Designated the Medina class, it was an experimental boat, nearly 40ft in length, and was considered to be an intermediate lifeboat; intermediate meant, according to the RNLI, a 'fast boat of about 35ft in length, essentially simple but with outstanding seakeeping qualities, which would bridge the gap between present offshore and inshore lifeboats to give greater flexibility in the provision of effective cover to all parts of the coast'.

The Medina was essentially an extension of the ideas embodied in the Atlantic 21. However, the Medina was powered by twin inboard diesel engines, rather than twin outboards as on the Atlantic. The hull had a vee-shaped cross-section forward for easy riding and good seakeeping, and included a bold sheer, with a flat area which assisted planing and kept the boat upright if grounded. Mounted on the rigid hull was the sponson, which was completely clear of the water when the boat was under way.

The prototype Medina, ON.1069, was built as an open boat, with self-righting capability provided by an inflatable air-bag fitted to a roll bar at the stern. A basic aluminium forward superstructure housed the steering position, and included a small shelter to take a stretcher and survivors. The second boat, ON.1072, had two different wheelhouses fitted during the course of its evaluation trials, as the first was found to be too small. The third boat, designated ON.1091, had a wheelhouse which was larger still, and incorporated an upper steering position.

Although the Medina hull form proved to be highly successful in extreme conditions, the large rigid inflatable performed very well in different sea states, the problems of finding suitable engines that were reliable yet of sufficiently low weight to be acceptable in the hull, were so great that the project was eventually abandoned. Numerous different

◀ The second Medina rigid inflatable, ON.1072, fitted with waterjets and pictured out of the water at the RNLI Depot, Poole. Following the RNLI's abandonment of the Medina design, the three boats were sold out of service. (Nicholas Leach)

▲ The KNRM's
Arie Visser type
rigid inflatable
is the service's
largest type,
measuring 18.8m
in length, 6.3m
in beam, and
displaces twenty-
eight tons, with a
speed of thirty-five
knots. The first of
these impressive
boats, class leader
Arie Visser, is
pictured departing
Terschelling, the
station she has
served since
October 1999.
(Nicholas Leach)

engine combinations were tried: the first Medina was powered initially by twin Sabre 212hp diesel engines, with power transmitted through twin Stern Powr type 83 outdrive units. At one stage three outboard units were fitted. The second boat was fitted with twin Volvo TAMD 60B engines and Volvo Type 750 outdrives, and the third boat, ON.1091, had Castoldi Type 06 waterjet units. None of these power units proved to be of sufficient strength, reliability and durability for rescue work, and the Medina concept was abandoned by the RNLI.

Despite the RNLI abandoning the Medina, various overseas lifeboat organisations went on to develop large rigid inflatables and operate them successfully. In 1983 the Norwegian Society for Sea Rescue built an 11.2m rigid inflatable, which had a speed of twenty-seven knots. In 1984 the Netherlands lifeboat society KZHMRS had a 12.6m rigid inflatable built, named Koningin Beatrix, which had an enclosed wheelhouse and served with distinction, and in 1986 the Canadian Coast Guard had a 14.2m rigid inflatable built. The Dutch went on to become the most successful proponents of the large rigid inflatable for rescue work. After the two previously independent Dutch lifeboat organisations merged in May 1991, to become the KNRM (Koninklijke Nederlandse Redding Maatschappij), the newly-unified organisation built and developed various rigid inflatable lifeboats of different sizes, and the country's fleet of offshore lifeboats consists entirely of fast rigid inflatables, with the largest measuring 18.8m in length.

Design and development

At the same time as the Medina was being trialled for possible service as an intermediate lifeboat, the RNLI was looking at commercial designs of small craft to assess their potential as lifeboats. The idea of an intermediate lifeboat stemmed from a perceived need to provide replacements for a small number of lifeboats at stations where the cost of a new offshore boat was considered to be unjustified on operational grounds, but where a lifeboat larger than the Atlantic 21 was deemed necessary.

In addition, it was determined that effective cover nearer to the coast needed to be strengthened as search and rescue requirements around the British Isles were changing. Faster offshore boats were frequently being called to go to casualties beyond the thirty-mile line used for operational planning purposes, so better cover closer to shore was considered necessary. The deployment of additional lifeboats to improve this cover could be achieved using a new type of intermediate boat: this

▼ The prototype Brede on trials. Based on the Lochin 33 design, the hull of which could be fitted out in single or twin screw versions as a workboat, fishing vessel or passenger launch, the RNLI version had a block mounted on the stern to provide a self-righting ability. (By courtesy of the RNLI)

would fill the gap between operational capabilities of the Atlantic 21 inshore lifeboat (a fast capable craft but with limited range) and the fast offshore lifeboats, such as the Aruns and Waveneys then in service.

The development project team set down a series of operational requirements for the proposed potential role of the new design, as follows:

(a) Dimensions: a maximum length of 35ft, with a beam of 14ft;

(b) Machinery, speed and endurance: propulsion from twin diesel inboard engines with electric starting, an operating speed of twenty-five knots, and endurance of six hours at operating speed, plus a twenty per cent safety margin;

(c) Night-time operations: full navigation lights, blue flashing light, portable search light, and chart table lighting; and

(d) Electronic equipment: VHF/FM radio, radar and echo sounder.

The design had to take into account the following requirements: (i) to operate in sea conditions greater than the limits laid down for the operation of inshore lifeboats, therefore able to operate in at least force eight conditions; (ii) to provide maximum safety for the crew, including having a self-righting capability and adequate shelter for crew and survivors; be suitable for operation by four crew, but capable of being operated by a reduced crew of three; (iii) to provide twenty-four-hour coverage with better capabilities than those offered by the existing A and B class ILBs (McLachlan 18 and Atlantic 21); (iv) to be launched by trolley from a slipway or beach, and to lie afloat, with the latter being the more important initial requirement; (v) to fulfil the following seagoing characteristics: have the ability to manoeuvre well; behave well in a seaway, particularly when running and operating at low speed; be of sufficient ruggedness to stand up to hard usage alongside and an occasional grounding; be easy to maintain and operate; and (vi) Operate within VHF range offshore; it was envisaged that under normal circumstances the new boat would have a maximum operating distance from the station of thirty miles.

CLASS NAME

Brede was chosen as the class name for the new lifeboat early in the design phase, conforming to what had become the RNLI's policy of naming modern lifeboats after the rivers or sailing waters near to where the first of the class was designed or built. The River Brede is a tributary of the River Rother, which flows into the sea at Rye, past Lochin Marine's boatyard.

BREDE LIFEBOATS

▲ The prototype 33ft Brede 33-01 on trials. The foam block at the stern gave the boat its self-righting capability, but was found to hinder rescue operations. This boat was used for trials only and never saw operational service. ◄

The RNLI's trials officer was briefed to make contact with boatbuilders, small boat fleet users and organisations including individual owners of small boats to assess suitable commercial designs which, with minimal modifications, would meet the operational requirements. This search was undertaken over eight months and involved interviews, discussions and sea trials with owners of craft of over fourteen different designs and

▶ The second Brede, Ann Ritchie, on trials in 1982 prior to going on station at Oban. She served at the Scottish station for only five years, as parts of her structure were weaker than required for use as a lifeboat and it was deemed more economical to dispose of her than undertake the necessary strengthening work. (By courtesy of the RNLI)

▶ Ann Ritchie was the first of the redesigned Bredes. Her layout was found to be suitable and so was used for all subsequent Bredes, with the large watertight wheelhouse providing the self-righting ability. (By courtesy of the RNLI)

applications. Two suitable designs were identified, but an attempt to acquire a two-month charter of each for further investigation proved difficult. It was therefore decided to order the more favoured commercial boat, the Lochin 33, from Lochin Marine of Rye and have it suitably adapted for trials with the RNLI's choice of machinery.

The Lochin 33 design was introduced in the early 1970s initially for use as a fishing boat by amateur sea anglers. When boatbuilder Frank Nichols (whose name is Lochin backwards) commissioned Robert Tucker to come up with her basic hull, he specified that she should be fast; that she should be as stable as possible, with a generous beam to length ratio; and that she should have good sea-keeping abilities at displacement and planing speeds. All of these qualities, desirable in a pleasure boat being used for sea angling, were also ideal for workboats, and the Lochin 33 was soon being used for commercial work having been adapted for a variety of purposes.

Well over 300 hulls were built to the basic design and Lochin craft were used extensively around the world, being found in Scandinavia, Northern Europe, the Mediterranean and America, as well as the British Isles. The design was eminently suitable not only for angling, but also for fishery patrol work, harbour launch work, as a fire tender and a small ferry. Among those authorities who operated Lochin 33 craft were the Swedish Navy, the Swedish Fire Service, Trinity House and the Gibraltar Police,

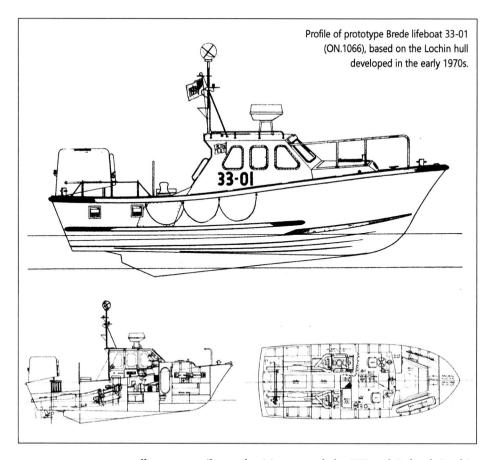

Profile of prototype Brede lifeboat 33-01 (ON.1066), based on the Lochin hull developed in the early 1970s.

as well as many pilot authorities around the UK and Ireland. Lochin Marine became known for high standards of construction, and the GRP techniques used for building the Lochin hulls were approved by Lloyds and Det Norske Veritas, as well as by the British White Fish Authority and the Department of Trade and Industry. Lochin prided itself on the skills of its shipwrights in fitting out the hulls.

Therefore, when the RNLI was reviewing available commercial hulls, the Lochin 33 was found to have the qualities being sought, and the design also had the advantage of being well tried in rough weather, so it was decided to evaluate a modified version of the boat in a lifeboat role. The selected boat, based on the hull designed by Robert Tucker, was moulded in GRP by Lochin Marine. The structural and interior design of the hull and superstructure to be assessed for suitability as

BREDE LIFEBOATS

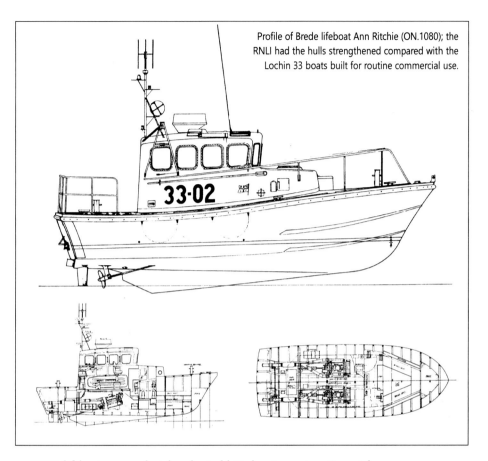

Profile of Brede lifeboat Ann Ritchie (ON.1080); the RNLI had the hulls strengthened compared with the Lochin 33 boats built for routine commercial use.

an RNLI lifeboat was undertaken by Judd Varley, in conjunction with Frank Nichols. The Brede lifeboat measured 33ft overall with a beam of 11ft 9in. A deep keel, sloping down aft to give a loaded draught 4ft 3in, was intended to give her good directional stability. In the boat's commercial applications, with a displacement of six tons and 360hp engines installed, a speed of twenty-five knots had been achieved.

The wheelhouse had sufficient space for a crew of four and seven survivors. The machinery, installed below the cockpit floor, was accessed by hatches which gave only limited space for routine inspection. Modifications needed to the hull, deck and superstructure stiffening were identified by the RNLI in conjunction with the builder, and the RNLI's preferred machinery of twin Caterpillar 3208NA engines was installed. The standard Lochin 33 had a large open cockpit aft and a

MACHINERY

■ Power for the Bredes came from twin Caterpillar 3208 naturally aspirated engines developing 203shp at 2,800rpm, through Twin Disc MG 506 gearboxes with 2:1 reduction. Ferralium 255 propeller shafts of 40mm diameter, supported by Cutless bearings in the stern tubes and A brackets, had aluminium bronze four-bladed propellers.

■ The exhaust system was water injected from the engine exhaust risers and had a continuous fall to the transom terminal fitted with a heat resistant rubber flap valve to prevent following seas entering the outlet. An Elastomuffle Type VII silencer was fitted in the exhaust system in the after fuel tank compartment.

■ Two separate stainless steel fuel tanks, each with a capacity of seventy-five gallons, were installed immediately forward and aft of the engine room. A Jabsco bilge pump was driven by each main engine through an electrically controlled clutch for pumping the engine room bilges. Other compartments were cleared of bilge water by a hand pump connected to a deck fitting.

■ The steering gear was a hand hydraulic system achieving full rudder travel with two and a half turns of the wheel. Bennett trim planes remotely controlled by the coxswain were fitted to the transom, with the actuating pumps installed in the steering compartment.

■ An automatic fire extinguishing system was installed in the engine room with a manually discharged second extinguisher situated outside the engine room. Portable BCF and foam extinguishers were also carried.

■ Two battery banks were fitted in the engine room, the engine starting bank with a capacity of seventy-five ampere hours and the boat load battery with a capacity of 190Ah. The batteries were connected for twenty-four-volt operation and could be cross coupled.

■ Electrical power was generated by a twenty-four ampere alternator driven by each main engine. A portable generator and a shore charging connection were provided for use when the main engines were not running. The main electrical distribution board was mounted in the wheelhouse and double pole circuit breakers were used throughout.

Dimensions and engines

The basic dimensions of all Bredes were the same. These details were published in The Lifeboat, Summer 1980, No.472, pp.48-50.

Length	33ft overall, 27ft 6in waterline
Maximum beam	12ft
Loaded draught	4ft 3in (aft)
Displacement	8.5 tons
Engines	Twin Caterpillar 3208 naturally aspirated marine diesels with twin disc MG506 2:1 reduction gearboxes
Power	203shp at 2,800rpm
Fuel capacity	182 gallons
Speed	Approx 20 knots maximum
Range	140 nautical miles at full speed
Crew	4

WHEELHOUSE AND CABIN

The wheelhouse had seated accommodation for four crew with good all-round visibility. The coxswain and radar operator/navigator had Bostrum sprung seats, and all seats had seatbelts. A basket stretcher, stowed inside the wheelhouse, was rigged at waist height when in use by a casualty. Three hinged noise insulated panels in the wheelhouse sole allowed access to the engine room beneath. Watertight doors led to the after deck and the forward survivor compartment.

The coxswain's console was provided with engine controls, a 21-inch steering wheel and a Sestrel Speed Major compass. Control switches for lighting, trim tabs and windscreen wipers and demisters were located on the inclined facia. The forward survivor compartment had bench seats for seven survivors with an escape hatch to the foredeck. A hot water boiler was provided along with stowage for freshwater containers.

◀ The fourth Brede, Philip Vaux (33-04), was stationed at Girvan on the Ayrshire coast. (By courtesy of the RNLI)

large open cockpit area aft. This area was initially deemed suitable for installing a roll bar fitted with an emergency airbag self-righting system. However, a large buoyancy block, mounted on a roll bar aft and made of polyurethane foam encapsulated in GRP, was incorporated into the Brede during construction after model testing indicated that self-righting was achievable with this block rather than fitted the airbag system. The block and watertight wheelhouse provided the boat's self-righting ability, which was proved when tested in a self-righting trial.

◀ Leonore Chilcott (33-03) approaches Fowey Town Quay for her naming ceremony on 26 April 1984, with the relief Brede Merchant Navy (33-05) moored nearby. (Paul Richards)

In laying up the GRP hull, a spray technique was used, making the process fast and continuous, and resulting in a finished structure deemed of high quality. The scantlings of the stock hull were sturdy, but for her lifesaving role the boat was strengthened: the frames, extended in 'hoops' around the superstructure where possible, were of polyurethane encapsulated in GRP; the longitudinals were hardwood and they, too, were encased in GRP; and the wheelhouse was stiffened with two stainless steel pillars, which also provided extra supports for the crew moving about when the boat was under way.

The hull was divided into five watertight compartments, with bulkheads of 19mm marine ply, and all void compartments within the hull were filled with polyurethane foam; in fact, the boat contained enough foam buoyancy to float even if all the watertight compartments should be flooded at the same time. Strengthening modifications added weight to the prototype, meaning it exceeded the design predictions, and the displacement of 9.6 tons was heavier than planned.

In designing the layout of the wheelhouse particular attention was paid to making sure that the crew would arrive at a casualty warm and dry and in the best possible shape and that survivors could be brought home with minimal further exposure. Sprung pedestal seats were installed for

▼ Merchant Navy (33-05) taking part in the International Lifeboat Conference in Sweden in 1985. The fifth Brede was built as a Relief lifeboat. (By courtesy of the RNLI)

BREDE LIFEBOATS

coxswain and navigator, with upholstered bench seats on the forward side of the main bulkhead for the two other crew members and two survivors; all seats had lap straps. There was a cabin for survivors forward of the wheelhouse, which was large enough to take a stretcher which could be carried below straight through the central watertight doors in the two bulkheads, and down into the fore cabin. The wheelhouse and fore cabin were both well ventilated, the vents all being fitted with valves which closed automatically should the boat be capsized. There was a compartment with a chemical toilet in the fore cabin and a water heater was fitted in the wheelhouse for preparing hot drinks.

With the design work complete, in February 1978 the RNLI placed the order for its prototype Brede (ON.1066) and the vessel was completed and delivered in January 1980 ready for trials. Initial trials undertaken by the boatbuilder revealed a number of aspects which negatively affected operational requirements. The maximum speed was only eighteen knots, due to the boat's displacement, running trim and propeller design, which prevented the engines reaching their rated speed. In addition, the standard spray rails failed to keep spray clear of the wheelhouse's forward windows in all but minimal seas.

A series of alterations were made to overcome these issues, including attempts to reduce the boat's weight. Improved spray rails were added to the hull, along with variable trim tabs, and propellers with more suitable characteristics were fitted. Further trials of the boat were

▶ Enid of Yorkshire (33-09) was the eighth Brede Mk.II and the second Brede to be built for service in the Relief Fleet. She is pictured on trials in 1984. (By courtesy of the RNLI)

carefully analysed to determine the optimum conditions to achieve the best performance. Lochin Marine provided comparative tests after constructing another boat for use as a general purpose launch, which incorporated many of the envisaged design modifications. This was used for trials in conjunction with the prototype so that improvements could be identified more precisely.

Trials of the prototype showed that the deck layout and overall configuration needed to be changed. Operational evaluation indicated

▶ The dedication ceremony of Nottinghamshire (33-10) at the Old Market Square, Nottingham on 28 April 1984. The boat had been funded by an appeal in the county and the unusual event, which saw the lifeboat coming inland, recognised the efforts of the fund-raisers. (Nicholas Leach)

that a larger wheelhouse was required and that the self-righting GRP-encapsulated foam block hindered rescue operations. A redesign of the deck and wheelhouse was therefore undertaken, and the after cockpit was dispensed with, leaving a flush deck. The wheelhouse was extended to fully cover the engine access hatches and fuel tanks, rearranged to compensate for changes to the centre of gravity, and modified so that it had greater headroom, incorporating rearward sloping forward windows. These changes gave the new design an inherent self-righting capability by virtue of the size of the watertight wheelhouse. The engine spacing was also reduced so that engine access was improved, and hinged engine access hatches were provided in the wheelhouse.

In December 1980 an order was placed for a modified version, designated the Brede Mk.II, which was very different from the prototype. Construction work on this second Brede (ON.1080) commenced in February 1981, and it was launched in October 1981 for trials, the first of which was a self-righting test in which the boat righted herself in just three seconds. During sea trials the boat performed very well and was found to be better than the prototype. Displacement had been reduced to 9.06 tons and speed increased to 18.7 knots. Although the

▲ Safeway (33-11), the penultimate Brede, on exercise at Calshot in August 1999. She served the station at the mouth of the Solent for almost seventeen years, launching more than 250 times on service. (By courtesy of the RNLI)

BREDE LIFEBOATS

increase was not very significant, it was an improvement. In addition, the wetness in the majority of sea conditions was resolved with a double spray rail configuration. After extensive sea trials, the boat was accepted by the RNLI in January 1982, and a further six months of trials followed.

As the Brede Mk.II proved to be a much better boat, in November 1981 orders were placed with Lochin Marine for two more boats (ON.1083 and ON.1084) to the Mk.II specification, with another four boats (ON.1087 to ON.1090) ordered in March 1982. Additional weight-saving measures were identified during the building of the second boat, but were prevented from being implemented by the need for production

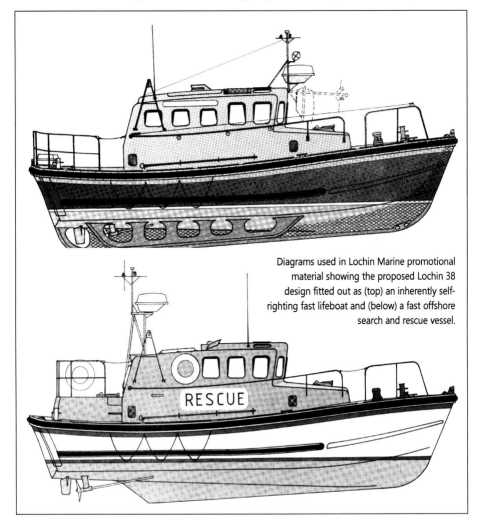

Diagrams used in Lochin Marine promotional material showing the proposed Lochin 38 design fitted out as (top) an inherently self-righting fast lifeboat and (below) a fast offshore search and rescue vessel.

retooling, so were only introduced with the third boat. These measures included closer control of the hull, deck and superstructure GRP layup, improvements to the wheelhouse and deck fastenings, and a reduction in weight of the wheelhouse sole and the noise insulation panels. The third boat of the class (ON.1083) had a displacement of 8.26 tons and achieved a speed of 20.28 knots during speed trials. The last four Bredes were completed in 1984 and 1985, with Calshot, on England's south coast, and Invergordon, in Scotland, identified as being suitable stations from where they could operate.

The development of the 33ft Brede for rescue work led the RNLI and Lochin Marine to examine whether it could be further adapted. The RNLI was looking for a new faster carriage-launched lifeboat design to replace the aging Oakleys and other displacement-hulled designs with a speed of less than nine knots that had been in service since the 1950s, and a Lochin design was considered. Lochin Marine added bilge keels to a standard Lochin 33, which was then used for carriage launching trials, but the RNLI chose to pursue its own design of carriage-launched lifeboat, the 12m (38ft) Mersey, which entered service in the late 1980s.

Lochin Marine also designed a 38ft version of the Lochin hull, and produced plans for the larger boat in a variety of uses and with different layouts and configurations. The larger Lochin was deemed to be suitable

▶ The Lochin type lifeboat Bernard Matthews, which measured 38ft 6in in length and 13ft in breadth, being recovered on the beach at Caister, where she served as a lifeboat for thirteen years until 2004. The boat's equipment included twin echo sounders, a survivors cabin for eight people, VHF direction finder, Decca navigator, fire-fighting equipment and cabin controls duplicated at the upper steering position. (Nicholas Leach)

as a lifeboat by the Caister Volunteer Rescue Service (CVRS) in Norfolk, an independent organisation, which was looking to acquire a new lifeboat in the 1980s. The CVRS purchased a 38ft 6in hull from Lochin Marine and contracted Goodchild Marine, based at Burgh Castle, to fit it out as a lifeboat, while another local firm, LEC Marine, agreed to carry out the electrical contract free of labour costs. Fitting out began on 26 September 1989 and, after the work had been completed at Goodchild's yard, the boat underwent a series of trials, arriving at Caister for the first time on 15 May 1991. Weighing twelve tons, she was powered by twin 280hp Ford Sabre diesel engines, which give her a speed of eighteen knots and a range of 220 nautical miles. She served at Caister until 2004.

At the time of their introduction, the Bredes were an innovative solution to meet the specific requirements of a few stations, which needed a fast boat, as the RNLI was looking to operate boats that were faster than the nine knots of existing displacement-hulled lifeboats. In terms of the RNLI's overall fleet development, the Brede also provided the opportunity to assess commercial third-party designs, while its use was also a relatively economical way of introducing a new lifeboat type, which was not only faster than older designs but was also self-righting. The introduction of the Bredes happened quite quickly, with the eleven boats that saw operational service completed within the space of just three years.

The stations where Brede lifeboats served were seen as being suitable for intermediate lifeboat operations, meaning certain limitations were

▼ Inner Wheel (33-07) served at Poole for almost eighteen years. (By courtesy of the RNLI)

placed on the boats and these needed to be recognised. Seven stations in total operated Bredes: Oban, Fowey, Girvan, Exmouth, Poole, Alderney, Calshot and Invergordon. Each had slightly unusual areas of operation, covering areas of relatively sheltered waters, where the type of rescues undertaken could be effected more efficiently with a faster lifeboat.

The first Brede to enter service, 33-02 (ON.1080), went to Oban on the west coast of Scotland in June 1982. She was named Ann Ritchie in recognition of the gift of Mrs J.B. Ritchie, who had already donated the 37ft Oakley James Ball Ritchie (ON.995) at Ramsey and the 54ft Arun The Gough Ritchie (ON.1051) at Port St Mary. At Oban, the eighteen-knot Brede replaced two lifeboats: the 42ft Watson Dorothy and Philip Constant (ON.967), a nine-knot displacement-hulled craft which was deemed too slow for undertaking rescues in an area getting ever busier with leisure craft, and the smaller 18ft 6in McLachlan A-511. During her evaluation period at Oban, Ann Ritchie operated with limitations on launches in severe weather while her capabilities were being assessed.

She carried out a fine service in the small hours of 31 January 1985 after the fishing vessel Shemara went aground on Lady's Rock, when her speed enabled a rescue to be carried out quickly and efficiently. The Oban crew was paged and at 3.32am and Ann Ritchie (33-02) put out, with Coxswain/Mechanic Patrick Maclean in command. Once clear of the harbour, the lifeboat headed north-west towards Lady's Rock at full speed, facing near gale force seven winds, gusting to gale force eight, with rough seas. Within twenty minutes of launching, the lifeboat arrived off Lady's Rock to find the fishing boat hard on the reef.

▶ Ann Ritchie, the first Brede to enter operational service, pictured at Oban during her stint there of just five years. (By courtesy of Oban RNLI)

BREDE LIFEBOATS

The lifeboat made the first of a series of runs to the fishing vessel's port quarter, with the coxswain placing the starboard shoulder of the lifeboat against the casualty. It took sixteen such runs to recover the eight people from the vessel. By 4.05am the rescue had been completed and an ambulance met the lifeboat on her return as the fishing boat's skipper was suffering from angina. For this service the Thanks of the Institution on vellum were awarded to Coxswain/Mechanic Patrick Maclean. Vellum service certificates were awarded to Assistant Mechanic David Graham and crew William Forteith and Michael Robertson.

▲ The second Brede to enter operational service, Leonore Chilcott, pictured at moorings off the Town Quay at Fowey. (Paul Richards)

The second Brede, Leonore Chilcott (33-03), went to Fowey in Cornwall, replacing a 46ft 9in Watson dating from the 1950s, while the third Brede was sent to Girvan in Ayrshire, to replace William and Mary Durham (ON.941), a 1957-built 42ft Watson. Michael Vlasto, the RNLI's Divisional Inspector for Scotland in the 1980s, took the Girvan boat, Philip Vaux (33-04), through the Irish Sea on her delivery passage in a force nine gale, with the boat reaching Dun Laoghaire, just south of Dublin, safely for an overnight stop. He recalled: 'she proved more than capable of handling such conditions and the heavy seas'. After her stop in Ireland, she reached Girvan, on the approaches to the Clyde.

At Exmouth, with Torbay's all-weather 54ft Arun class lifeboat just fourteen nautical miles away for coverage in extreme weather, Caroline Finch (33-06) was placed on station in August 1983. She replaced the 48ft 6in Solent City of Birmingham (ON.1012), a steel-hulled lifeboat with a speed of nine knots, which had been at Exmouth since 1970. The Brede served for almost eleven years, launching 178 times on service.

Before she reached her station, Caroline Finch undertook a fine rescue. On 5 June 1983, in rain squalls, she was returning to Poole after engine trials with Staff Coxswain Edward Mallinson in command. A yacht was firing distress flares south of St Albans Head in near gale force seven winds from the north-east, gusting to severe gale force nine, with rough seas. The Brede set off to help at full speed, and found the 33ft sloop Junio heading south under engine power, with her sails split and two people on board. The lifeboat led the yacht out of the overfalls on St Albans Ledge then, with another severe squall approaching from the west, Exmouth Assistant Mechanic Timothy Mock was put aboard. He stowed the sails and took over the helm just before the squall struck, which saw the vessel face force nine westerly winds and hail. Both boats maintained steerage until the squall had moderated, and then the lifeboat escorted the yacht into Poole Harbour.

▼ The champagne smashes over the bow of Caroline Finch (33-06) at the end of her naming ceremony at Exmouth on 24 July 1984.

The stations at Calshot and Poole on England's south coast were also ideal for intermediate operations, with Calshot covering the Solent and Southampton Water, while Poole station's patch included the large natural harbour, which was sheltered but very busy with leisure and commercial craft. Poole was served by Inner Wheel (33-07) for eighteen years, during which time she is credited with over 800 service launches. Two Bredes were stationed successively at Calshot over a period totalling seventeen years. These two stations, along with Oban, were served by Bredes for the longest period.

The third station in Scotland to be served by a Brede was Invergordon, in the north-west, which covered the sheltered Firths of Cromarty, Moray and Dornoch. Just reaching the open sea from the berth involved a passage of about seven miles along the Cromarty Firth. The speedy Brede replaced a nine-knot 52ft Barnett, James and Margaret Boyd (ON.913), at the station, which had only been established in 1974, but the Brede herself remained for only four years.

A somewhat unusual place to be chosen for intermediate lifeboat operations was Alderney in the Channel Islands. The RNLI had decided

▲ Foresters Future (33-08) served as the first lifeboat at Alderney when the station was re-established in 1984. She later spent sixteen years in the Relief Fleet. (By courtesy of the RNLI)

to establish a new station on the island and the Brede Foresters Future (33-08) was sent there in March 1984 for an initial trial period of twelve months. The local people placed their wholehearted support behind the establishment of the new station and recruiting a crew proved straightforward. The most northerly of the Channel Islands, Alderney had seen the number of visiting yachts calling at Braye Harbour greatly increase, while the RNLI lifeboat at neighbouring Guernsey had helped an increasing number of yachts and fishing vessels in the area, indicating the need for the new station. Foresters Future arrived in Alderney on 28 January 1984, and after a period of crew training overseen by Inspector Les Vipond or his deputy Chris Price, she was placed on station on 10 March 1984.

The decision to establish the station was soon justified when, on 4 May 1986, the lifeboat was involved in an outstanding service, rescuing four people from the yacht Sea Victor in southerly gale-force winds and extremely rough seas. The yacht was also saved, and the service resulted in the Bronze medal being awarded to Coxswain Stephen Shaw, with the Thanks of the Institution on Vellum being accorded to Mechanic Michael O'Gorman. Another medal-winning service was performed by the Alderney crew on 25 August 1986, when the lifeboat rescued six people and saved the yacht Seylla II, which was in difficulty in southerly storm force ten conditions. Further Bronze medals were awarded, this time to both Coxswain Shaw and Second Coxswain Martin Harwood.

A fine service by the Brede at Exmouth was undertaken during the evening of 20 November 1986. A machinery failure and broken anchor cable aboard the trawler Brigg left her drifting helplessly south east of Otter Point, South Devon, in westerly force six winds and rough seas. Caroline Finch, with Second Coxswain/Mechanic Timothy Mock at the wheel, was be sent to help and found the trawler less than two miles offshore and being blown steadily towards rocks. A line was passed and the vessel was towed away from danger and back to Exmouth Docks, with the return passage of five nautical miles lasting almost three hours. The towline parted five times on the way, but was reconnected each time. In his report, Deputy Divisional Inspector Peter Bradley, commented: 'The persistence and skill shown by Second Coxswain Mock and his crew in towing the Brigg from a lee shore to the safety of the Harbour, is worthy of note, particularly as the tow parted on numerous occasions'. A letter of appreciation signed by the director, Rear Admiral W. J. Graham, was sent to Second Coxswain/Mechanic Mock and his crew, congratulating them on their seamanship and perseverance.

Replacements

Experience showed that at some of the stations initially deemed suitable for intermediate operations, the Bredes were not ideal as the weather limitations place on them reduced their overall effectiveness. At Alderney, where services often involved facing heavy seas and travelling long distances, the Brede was replaced after just two and a half years by a 44ft Waveney, while Leonore Chilcott (33-03) lasted just over five years at Fowey. At Invergordon, Nottinghamshire (33-10) spent just four

◀ The last Brede to enter service, Amateur Swimming Associations (33-12) ,was built for the Relief Fleet but served for four years at Girvan, which had all-weather lifeboats at its neighbouring stations.

years in service. However, at three stations, Poole, Calshot and Oban, the Brede proved to be an ideal type of lifeboat.

The Bredes at Alderney, Exmouth, Invergordon and Fowey were replaced by 44ft Waveneys, none of which was new when the changeover occurred, whereas the Brede at Poole, which had replaced a Waveney, was itself replaced by a 47ft Tyne. Oban was served by three different Bredes, the last of which, Nottinghamshire (33-10), was replaced by a new 14m Trent, Mora Edith Macdonald (ON.1227), in 1997. A 12m Mersey, Silvia Burrell (ON.1196), took over from the second of the two Bredes to serve at Girvan. At Calshot a 52ft Arun took over in April 2002, replacing the last Brede in RNLI service, Inner Wheel (33-07).

The Bredes proved to be something of an anomaly and, by the end of the 1990s, with the RNLI looking to consolidate the fleet and reduce the number of different lifeboat classes, they were replaced. The Brede was one of very few commercial designs to have been used by the RNLI, as in-house designs which replaced Bredes were favoured. An exception came in the early years of the twenty-first century when the RNLI established a rescue service on the Thames with boats designed by a third party.

BREDE LIFEBOATS

Brede lifeboats: after service

The length of operational service of the eleven Brede lifeboats built for the RNLI varied considerably. The first four boats, 33-02, 33-03, 33-04 and 33-05, had short careers after issues with their hulls were found and they were taken out of service, but the subsequent boats gave much longer service. While the first of the Mk.II Bredes, 33-02, was broken up at Dumbarton, the next two, 33-03 and 33-04, were sold out of service in 1990 and ended up as pilot boats, at Alderney and Carlingford respectively. All the other boats ended up serving overseas as lifeboats, with all but one in South Africa. The other Brede to be sold in 1990, 33-05, was used initially as a pleasure boat at Groningen and then on the south coast of England, but, perhaps unsurprisingly, she also ended up in South Africa.

In total, seven Bredes were operated by the National Sea Rescue Institute (NSRI) and they were very well liked in South Africa, giving exceptional service and saving a huge number of lives off the South African coast.

◀ 33-03 out of the water at the RNLI Depot, Poole in August 1990, with her markings removed, prior to being sold. She was initially used as a diving/ survey boat at Littlehampton before being bought in August 1999 by Alderney Pilots for about £35,000. (Nicholas Leach)

▲ 33-07 out of the water at the RNLI Depot in Poole (left) in July 2002 shortly after being sold out of service to the NSRI. She was renamed Nadine Gordimer in South Africa (right) and served as Rescue 8 at Hout Bay.

In fact, they have given more years of life-saving service in the southern hemisphere than they did with the RNLI. They were operated from seven different stations, three of which (Hout Bay, Gordon's Bay, and Simon's Town) were located near Cape Town on the country's south-western coast. From west to east, the other stations with Bredes were Hermanus, on the southern coast of the Western Cape province; Port Elizabeth, a city on Algoa Bay, covering the waters of the Eastern Cape; and Durban, the most easterly station to be served by a Brede.

The Bredes Rescue 15 at Mossel Bay, Rescue 17 at Hermanus, Rescue 10 at Simon's Town and Rescue 6 at Port Elizabeth were launched from a cradle winched down a slipway. This launch method meant the boat

Bredes in service with NSRI, South Africa

Name	ON	Built	NSRI	Station	Notes
Rescue 15	1087	1983	2012	Rescue 15, Mossel Bay	Refitted along with Hout Bay's Nadine Gordimer; returned to the water on 6 November 2012
South Star	1088	1983	1994	Rescue 17, Hermanus	
Nadine Gordimer	1089	1983	2002	Rescue 8, Hout Bay	Refit started in March 2012 and completed on 20 February 2013
Spirit of Safmarine III	1090	1984	2002	Rescue 10, Simon's Town	
Spirit of Toft	1101	1984	1997	Rescue 6, Port Elizabeth	
Sanlam Rescuer	1102	1984	1997	Rescue 9, Gordon's Bay	Destroyed by fire whilst awaiting refit in a boat building factory in December 2010
Eikos Rescuer II	1104	1985	2002	Rescue 5, Durban	Decommissioned June 2019, sold and renamed Boss Charger

◄ 33-05 was sold out of service in 1990 and became a private pleasure boat named Lyonesse. In 2012 she was bought by the NSRI at a cost of £55,000 to replace 33-10, which had been destroyed in a fire. She is pictured at Lochin Marine in January 2012 on her shipping cradle, just prior to being shipped via Tilbury Docks to South Africa. (By courtesy of NSRI)

◄ 33-05 arrived in South Africa in February 2012 and, after a major refit, became Rescue 15 and was stationed at Mossel Bay. (By courtesy of the NSRI)

◄ 33-11 in service at Durban as Rescue 5. She was operated from the city, in eastern South Africa's KwaZulu-Natal province, from 2002 until 2019. (By courtesy of the NSRI)

▶ The only Brede to serve overseas as a lifeboat but not in South Africa was 33-12, which was renamed Sealord Rescue for Coastguard service at Port Nelson, New Zealand, where she is pictured with three former RNLI 44ft Waveneys, which had also been sold to New Zealand. (By courtesy of the RNLI)

▼ 33-03 in Braye Harbour, Alderney close to the operational RNLI lifeboat, a 14m Trent. She is one of two Bredes later used as pilot boats. (Nicholas Leach)

could be housed, enabling maintenance work to be carried out more easily and protecting the boat from the elements. The NSRI had the Bredes refitted a number of times, but by the 2020s they were starting to be phased out and replaced by ORC 140 type craft, a 14m all-weather self-righting rescue vessel which was based on a design from the French lifeboat society Société Nationale de Sauvetage en Mer (SNSM). The first of the NSRI's Bredes to be decommissioned, 33-11, was taken out of service in June 2019 and sold to a private owner.

Careers of the Bredes

O f the twelve Brede lifeboats that were built, eleven saw life-saving service with the RNLI; the prototype was used only for trials, after which it was sold. The first three Bredes to become operational served their stations for six years or less. However, subsequent boats went on to have much longer careers, and the Brede design proved to be particularly suited to the stations at Poole and Calshot on the south coast, both of which were served by Bredes for more than seventeen years, and Oban on the west coast of Scotland.

The introduction of the Bredes happened quite quickly, and proved to be an economical way of bringing in a new design at a time when the RNLI was seeking to operate a fleet of self-righting lifeboats which were also faster then the conventional nine-knot boats. The Bredes certainly filled a gap in the RNLI fleet, and in this section details of each boat, with information about its subsequent career, can be found.

▼ Exmouth's Brede Caroline Finch (33-06) moored in the River Exe on 24 July 1984 during the celebrations to mark her naming ceremony. (By courtesy of the RNLI)

Un-named (33-01)

Key data

BUILT 1982, Lochin Marine, Rye, Sussex
STATIONS Trials 1980 – 1982
RECORD No services
DISPOSAL Sold on 20 January 1983 to David Lemonius, Yarmouth, IOW

Service history

33-01 was the prototype Brede and was used by the RNLI only for trials, over the course of about three years, and she was never formally named. The boat had a different layout and deck configuration, which meant she was unsuitable for rescue work. The trials proved the viability of the hull, and the need to redesign the deck layout.

After service

33-01 was sold out of service in January 1983 following the completion of trials. She was acquired by David Lemonius who renamed her *John Alexander* and used her as a work boat at Yarmouth, IOW, where she was moored in the harbour. The buoyancy block at the stern was removed but the boat otherwise remained unaltered. She remained on the Isle of Wight for more than two decades. In June 1999 she came to Poole and took part in the RNLI's 175th anniversary parade, being used as a camera boat during the event. In about 2007 she was moved to Cowes, being kept moored on the east side of the river Medina in front of the old Vosper's yard. In about 2011 David Lemonius sold her to Blade Runner Shipping, of Southampton, who refitted the boat before using her as a work boat. She was sometimes moored at Venture Quays, Cowes but was usually kept in a cradle at Blade Runner's main premises in Southampton's Eastern Docks' Berth 24/25, being launched when required.

▲ The prototype Brede 33-01 on trials, with the superstructure based on a standard Lochin 33 design.

▲ 33-01 owned by Blade Runner Shipping, at Southampton, June 2012. (Nicholas Leach)

Ann Ritchie (33-02)

Key data

BUILT 1982, Lochin Marine, Rye, Sussex
DONOR Gift of Mrs Ann A. Ritchie, Isle of Man.
STATIONS Oban Jun 1982 – Sep 1987
RECORD 186 launches, 20 lives saved
DISPOSAL Scrapped in January 1988 at Dumbarton

Service history

ANN RITCHIE was the first production Brede, and undertook her initial trials during January and February 1982, completing her final trials out of Rye between 8 and 11 February. She was then taken to the RNLI Depot at Poole, where she underwent further trials, which included passages to St Peter Port (Guernsey) in early March 1982, Yarmouth and Weymouth, and Newhaven, returning to Rye for maintenance and overhaul in May 1982. She was allocated to Oban, whose crew undertook training on the boat in early June 1982, after which she was sailed to her station. The passage involved stops at Plymouth, Newlyn, Padstow, Milford Haven, Arklow, Holyhead, Port St Mary, Portpatrick, Campbeltown and Oban, where she arrived on 10 June 1982. She was named at Oban on 7 May 1983 by the donor, Mrs Ann Ritchie, becoming the third lifeboat given to the RNLI by Mrs Ritchie following the 37ft Oakley James Ball Ritchie (Ramsey) and the 54ft Arun The Gough Ritchie (Port St Mary). In attendance at the naming ceremony were Frank Nichols, the owner of Lochin Marine, and P. Denham Christie, who had chaired the RNLI Boat Committee during the introduction of the Brede class into the fleet. Ann Ritchie served at Oban for just five years, during which she proved to be much in demand, undertaking almost 200 services.

After service

ANN RITCHIE was replaced at Oban in 1987 by another Brede, Merchant Navy (33-05), after an RNLI hull inspector found that her hull had become saturated with water, which did not dry when the boat was taken out for a bottom scrub and anti-fouling. She was taken to McAlister's Boatyard at Dumbarton, initially for storage, but eventually a decision was made to scrap her hull as undertaking the necessary remedial work to the GRP was deemed to be uneconomic, and she was broken up in January 1988.

▲ 33-02 at Oban in July 1983 at the start of her career. (Tony Denton)

▲ 33-02 during her time at Oban, which lasted only five years. (By courtesy of the RNLI)

Leonore Chilcott (33-03)

Key data

BUILT 1982, Lochin Marine, Rye, Sussex
DONOR Gift of Paul Chilcott, Guernsey, in memory of his wife
STATIONS Fowey Oct 1982 – Jan 1988
RECORD 57 launches, 19 lives saved
DISPOSAL Sold on 30 September 1990 to Barry and Vivian Meredith, Newport Pagnell

Service history

LEONORE CHILCOTT was on trails out of the RNLI Depot, Poole during September 1982, followed by crew training. Her passage to Fowey was undertaken between 24 and 29 September, when she reached her station. After further crew training, she was declared operational on 16 October 1982. She was named and dedicated on 26 April 1984 at the Town Quay, Fowey, by Paul Chilcott, in memory of his late wife. She was fairly busy performing numerous services to dinghies, yachts and other pleasure craft, and she launched a total of fifty-seven times on service. However, she did not serve at Fowey for long, just over five years, before being replaced by the 44ft Waveney Thomas Forehead and Mary Rowse II (ON.1028), which had been stationed at Plymouth, in January 1988. Leonore Chilcott was to be used as a Relief lifeboat, but in February 1988, after she had been taken to Branksea Marine, Wareham, it was discovered that her scantlings were too light for the necessary hull re-skimming using the standard repair system. As a result, in October 1989 it was determined that hull remedial work was not viable, so she was taken to the RNLI Depot at Poole, stored ashore, and offered for sale.

After service

LEONORE CHILCOTT was replaced at Fowey in January 1988 and taken to Branksea Marine, Wareham, and then to the RNLI Depot at Poole, from where she was sold out of service in September 1990. She was renamed Privateer by her new owners and, largely unaltered, was based at Littlehampton Marina, being used as a diving and survey boat during the 1990s. In August 1999 she was bought by Alderney Pilots for approximately £35,000 and, after being overhauled, was taken to the Channel Islands for use as the main pilot cutter at Alderney, based in Braye Harbour. She initially had a black hull and red superstructure, but this was later changed to light grey. She has been used as the pilot boat at Alderney for more than twenty years.

▲ 33-03 in the estuary at Fowey, the station she served for six years. (Nicholas Leach)

▲ 33-03 moored at Alderney, in use as a pilot boat, with her lifeboat name, September 2018. (Nicholas Leach)

Key data

BUILT 1982, Lochin Marine, Rye, Sussex

DONOR Provided by Mrs Elizabeth Felicity Vaux in memory of her husband Cdr P.E. Vaux, DSC RN, who served as the RNLI's Chief Inspector of Lifeboats from 1939 to 1951, and their son Lt Cdr M.P. Vaux, DSC RN

STATIONS Girvan Feb 1983 – Apr 1989

RECORD 57 launches, 17 lives saved

DISPOSAL Sold out of service in May 1990 to RTK Marine/Mosely Holdings

Service history

PHILIP VAUX was completed in January 1983 and, following acceptance and engine trials, was taken to the RNLI Depot at Poole. Crew training for the Girvan crew was undertaken in late January 1983, after which the new boat was taken north, with the passage including stops at Falmouth on 5 February and Donaghadee two days later; she arrived at Girvan on 8 February 1983, and was immediately being placed on station. Philip Vaux was formally christened at Girvan on 25 June 1983 by Harry Vaux, Cdr Philip Vaux's brother. She was named after the donor's husband, Philip E. Vaux, formerly the RNLI Chief Inspector of Lifeboats, and her son, Lt Cdr M.P. Vaux. Philip Vaux undertook her first service on 3 April 1983, but, after just six years at the Ayrshire station, she was replaced by another Brede, Amateur Swimming Associations. On 12 April 1989 she was taken to McAlister's Boatyard at Sandpoint, Dumbarton, where it was found the scantlings were too light for the hull. Re-skinning with the standard repair system was deemed not to be viable.

After service

PHILIP VAUX was stored at McAlister's Boatyard from 12 April to October 1989, when she was moved to the RNLI Depot at Poole. As the necessary remedial work was not viable, the boat was placed on the sale list on 4 October 1989 and in May 1990 was sold out of service for £32,500. She was used as a work boat based at Hamworthy, Poole, for a number of years during the early 1990s, having been renamed RTK Sea Truck 4. In about 1993 she was sold and taken to Carlingford Lough where, renamed Mourne Mist, she took up duties as Carlingford pilot boat No.1, remaining largely unaltered externally.

▲ 33-04 on station at Girvan. (By courtesy of the RNLI)

▲ 33-04, renamed Mourne Mist, at Greencastle as a pilot boat, April 2015. (Nicholas Leach)

Merchant Navy (33-05)

Key data

BUILT 1983, Lochin Marine, Rye, Sussex
DONOR Merchant Navy Appeal
STATIONS Relief Apr 1983 – 1987; Oban Sep 1987 – Mar 1989
RECORD 34 launches, 10 lives saved (Relief); 73 launches, 11 lives saved (Oban)
DISPOSAL Sold on 6 June 1990 to Gerrit Gerritsen, Holwierde, Netherlands

Service history

MERCHANT NAVY was built as a Relief lifeboat and completed her acceptance trials on 28 and 29 March 1983, after which she entered the Relief Fleet, going to Alderney for trials on 12 April 1983 and undertaking her first Relief duties at Exmouth starting on 20 April 1983. In May 1983 she was sailed to Gothenburg, Sweden to take part in the International Lifeboat Conference, arriving on 5 June 1983 and staying for five days, returning to the RNLI Depot at Poole on 20 June 1983. She was named on 19 October 1983 at St Katharine Docks, London, by Dr Ronald Hope, Director of the Marine Society, with representatives in attendance from all parts of the merchant service and their maritime colleagues. The boat was named to mark the contributions of merchant seamen to RNLI funds. She undertook Relief duties at Oban and Girvan in late 1983, and during 1984 and 1985 served Fowey, Exmouth, Poole, Alderney and Calshot at various times on Relief. In August 1987 she was taken by road to McAlister's Boatyard at Dumbarton and reallocated to Oban on temporary station duty, where she stayed for eighteen months.

After service

MERCHANT NAVY was sold out of service in June 1990 to an owner in the Netherlands, and was used as a pleasure boat at Delfzijl Marina, Groningen. In 2006 she was bought by Alan Lowe, of Surrey, and, renamed Lyonesse, returned to the UK to be moored in the River Hamble near Warsash. She later moved to Newhaven to be used as a pleasure boat, and was maintained in good condition. In 2012 the National Sea Rescue Institute of South Africa acquired her as a replacement lifeboat for the Brede 33-10, which had been destroyed in a fire in December 2010. In January 2012 Lyonesse was shipped from Tilbury Docks to Cape Town at no cost to the NSRI. She arrived on 1 February, was refitted with NSRI rescue equipment and resprayed in NSRI livery during an extensive overhaul at Cape Town, entering servce as Rescue 15 at Mossel Bay in November 2012, to become the seventh Brede operated by NSRI.

▲ 33-05 moored at St Katharine Docks in London for her naming ceremony in October 1983.

▲ 33-05 as Rescue 15 on station at Mossel Bay in South Africa, where she has served since 2012.

Caroline Finch (33-06)

Key data

BUILT 1983, Lochin Marine, Rye

DONOR Bequest of Mr W.H. Finch in memory of his mother Caroline; Mr H.E. Rohll in memory of his wife Hibby; Mr W.J. Orley and Mrs M.G. Shaw in memory of her husband Eric Baden Shaw; together with other gifts

STATIONS Exmouth Aug 1983 – Jun 1994

RECORD 178 launches, 64 lives saved

DISPOSAL Sold in 1994 to the National Sea Rescue Institute, South Africa

Service history

CAROLINE FINCH was built in early 1983, undertaking her self-righting trials programme in March 1983. Her main trials took place between 28 April and 13 May, with final trials at the end of May 1983. Crew training for the Exmouth volunteers was undertaken during June 1983, and while on passage to Jersey on 18 June she assisted the trawler Lady Crab, of Guernsey. After further training, she was placed on operational duty at Exmouth on 4 August 1983. Her naming ceremony was held at Exmouth Docks on 24 July 1984, when Their Royal Highnesses The Duke and Duchess of Kent came to name the boat, with the Duchess tasked with performing the formal christening. During just over a decade of service at Exmouth, Caroline Finch was launched 178 times on service, and performed some notable rescues. On 7 April 1985 she and her crew rescued a speedboat's three occupants after it had sunk in heavy seas and strong winds, for which the Thanks of the Institution Inscribed on Vellum were accorded to crew member Geoffrey Ingram. Another fine service took place on 21 June 1985, when the yacht Vamoss II, with two people on board, was towed to safety in gale-force winds, a rescue for which Second Coxswain/Mechanic Tim Mock received a letter of appreciation signed by the Chief of Operations. During 1989-90 the boat was taken to West Custom Marine for completion of re-skinning.

After service

CAROLINE FINCH was replaced at Exmouth in July 1994 and taken to the RNLI Depot, Poole, and sold to the National Sea Rescue Institute of South Africa. During August 1994 she was repainted in NSRI colours and on 26 August was transported to Tilbury Docks for shipment to South Africa. Renamed South Star, she was stationed at Rescue Station 17 in Hermanus, covering the seas between Gordon's Bay and Mossel Bay. The Station Committee raised R20,000 to extend the boathouse to accommodate the boat.

▲ 33-06 on exercise during her time at Exmouth, where she served for just over a decade.

▲ 33-06 on station at Hermanus as Rescue 17, named South Star.

Inner Wheel (33-07)

Key data

BUILT 1982, Lochin Marine, Rye, Sussex
DONOR Gift of Inner Wheel Clubs of Great Britain and Ireland, plus other gifts
STATIONS Poole Oct 1983 – Sep 2001; Calshot Dec 2001 – Apr 2002
RECORD 812 launches, 176 lives saved (Poole); 3 launches, 0 lives saved (Calshot)
DISPOSAL Sold in June 2002 to NSRI, South Africa without engines

Service history

INNER WHEEL was completed in September 1983 and after acceptance trials went to Poole, where crew training was undertaken between 30 September and 2 October 1983. She went on to serve at Poole as station lifeboat for eighteen years, undertaking more than 800 service launches during that time, making her the busiest of any of the Bredes. The cost of the lifeboat was met by an appeal organised by the Association of Inner Wheel Clubs in Great Britain and Ireland, together with other gifts and legacies. Her naming ceremony was held at the Town Quay, Poole, on 13 June 1984, when Mrs A.W. Brown, JP, past president of the Association of Inner Wheel Clubs, formally christened the boat. On of the highlights of Inner Wheel's career at Poole came in June 1999, when she took part in the Lifeboat Flotilla to mark the RNLI's 175th Anniversary. After being replaced at Poole by 47ft Tyne class lifeboat City of Sheffield (ON.1131) in early September 2001, she served at Calshot for five months as a Relief lifeboat, being replaced in April 2002 when she became the last 33ft Brede to leave active service.

After service

INNER WHEEL was replaced at Calshot in April 2002 and taken to the RNLI Depot, Poole, from where she was sold out of service to the National Sea Rescue Institute of South Africa in June 2002. She left Poole without engines on 19 January 2003, and was shipped to South Africa from Sheerness, leaving on 26 February 2003. She did not enter life-saving service until 2007, when, after extensive fund-raising, she was refitted and re-engined, being renamed Nadine Gordimer. She served at Station 8 Hout Bay, which has been in operation since 1979, and is located in Hout Bay Harbour, near Cape Town.

BREDE LIFEBOATS

▲ 33-07 on station at Poole, where she was the busiest of any of the Bredes. (John Buckby)

▲ After being sold out of service, 33-07 was taken to South Africa to continue her life-saving career, being renamed Spirit of Nadine Gordimer. She then became MTU Nadine Gordimer and served at Hout Bay.

Foresters Future (33-08)

Key data

BUILT 1983, Lochin Marine, Rye, Sussex

DONOR Ancient Order of Foresters to commemorate their 150th anniversary, and others

STATIONS Alderney Mar 1984 – Oct 1986; Relief Oct 1986 – 2002

RECORD 70 launches, 74 lives saved (Alderney); 201 launches, 35 lives saved (Relief)

DISPOSAL Sold in June 2002 to NSRI, South Africa without engines.

Service history

FORESTERS FUTURE was funded by the Belsize Charitable Trust No.1 and M.V. Hillhouse Trust, and the Ancient Order of Foresters, together with other contributions. She was built during 1983 and in December 1983 was taken to the RNLI Depot at Poole for final acceptance. After the new boat had completed trials during January 1984, crew training with the Alderney volunteers started. The Channel Islands station had been newly established, and Foresters Future was its first lifeboat, arriving there in February 1984 and being declared operational on 10 March 1984 for twelve months' station evaluation. She was brought to Poole on 18 July 1984 so that she could be named at a ceremony held on 19 July 1984, the first day of RNLI Open Days in Poole, which enabled members of the public to see the work of the RNLI. The new lifeboat was christened by Mrs Renee Roddie, wife of the Ancient Order of Foresters' High Chief Ranger, marking the Order's 150th anniversary. On 20 July 1984 she returned to Alderney for a further two years, proving the need for the new Channel Islands station by performing many fine rescues. In October 1986 she was replaced by a 44ft Waveney and was then reallocated to the Relief Fleet, in which she served for a further sixteen years undertaking duties mainly at Calshot and Poole, being based at the RNLI Depot.

After service

FORESTERS FUTURE was sold out of service in June 2002 to NSRI, South Africa, without engines. She left Poole on 19 January 2003, and was shipped to South Africa from Sheerness the following month. After extensive fund-raising to pay for new engines, she was renamed Spirit of Safmarine III and allocated to Rescue Station No.3 at Table Bay, moving in about 2007 to Rescue Station No.10 at Simon's Town, South Africa.

▲ 33-08 on relief duty at Calshot in February 1995. (Nicholas Leach)

▲ 33-08 renamed Spirit of Safmarine III, serving as Rescue Station No.3 at Table Bay in South Africa.

Enid of Yorkshire (33-09)

Key data

BUILT 1984, Lochin Marine, Rye, Sussex
DONOR Gift of Mr Arnold T. Sanderson, North Ferriby, East Yorkshire
STATIONS Relief Apr 1984 – Sept 1997
RECORD 113 launches, 12 lives saved
DISPOSAL Sold in October 1997 to NSRI, South Africa

Service history

ENID OF YORKSHIRE was built during 1983 and 1984, undertaking her self-righting trials programme in February 1984 at Alford's Wharf, Rye. Further trials in March 1984 were followed by final trials in April 1984, after which she entered the Relief Fleet having been delivered to the RNLI Depot, Poole. Funded by Arnold Sanderson, she was named on 22 June 1984 at Bridlington, having been taken to Yorkshire by road. She was christened by Mrs Muriel Fox, the donor's sister, after being formally handed over to the RNLI by his brother, Noel Sanderson. After her naming, she was taken by road to McAlister's Boatyard at Dumbarton, and then undertook Relief duties at Oban, Invergordon and Girvan during the 1980s and 1990s. Her sole Relief duty at Calshot was undertaken between May and November 1989, but the majority of her RNLI career was spent at the stations in Scotland which were served by Bredes.

After service

ENID OF YORKSHIRE was sold out of service in October 1997 to the National Sea Rescue Institute of South Africa. She was shipped to South Africa, where she operated from NSRI Station 6 at Port Elizabeth, covering Algoa Bay. She has been painted in new colours at the RNLI Depot, Poole prior to her departure, and was renamed Spirit of Toft for service in South Africa in honour of the late Tommy Toft, who was instrumental in raising the funds necessary for her purchase by the NSRI. In 2011 Spirit of Toft underwent a total refit at Durban, which was partly sponsored by Safmarine, who transported the boat from Port Elizabeth to Durban in February. The refit took about five months and involved installing new electrical equipment and repainting, returning her to station 'as good as new'. She has served in South Africa for more than twenty years.

▲ 33-09 on relief duty at Oban, July 1995. (Nicholas Leach)

▲ 33-09 was renamed Spirit of Toft and served as Rescue 6 at Port Elizabeth, Algoa Bay.

Nottinghamshire (33-10)

Key data
BUILT 1984, Lochin Marine, Rye, Sussex
DONOR Nottinghamshire Lifeboat Appeal 1982-84.
STATIONS Invergordon Jul 1984 – Jul 1988; Oban Mar 1989 – Jul 1997
RECORD 21 launches, 6 lives saved (Invergordon); 503 launches, 30 lives saved (Oban)
DISPOSAL Sold in December 1997 to NSRI, South Africa

Service history
NOTTINGHAMSHIRE was built during the first half of 1984, and was taken to Nottingham for a dedication ceremony on 28 April 1984 at Market Square in recognition of the appeal which had funded her. She completed her trials during June 1984, with a passage from Poole to Invergordon between 6 and 13 July. She was placed on station at Invergordon on 16 July 1984, after a short period of crew training. She was named at Invergordon on 4 May 1985 by Mrs Denis Wakeling, JP, wife of the appeal committee president, and dedicated by the Rt Rev Denis Wakeling. After four years at Invergordon, she was reallocated to Oban, being taken to Herd & Mackenzie's yard at Buckie for survey and overhaul. Declared operational at Oban on 28 March 1989, she became the third of three Bredes to serve the Scottish west coast station. She spent eight years at Oban, being replaced by the 14m Trent Mora Edith MacDonald (ON.1227) in July 1997. In September 1997 she was taken to Silvers Marine, Rosneath and stored prior to being taken by road to the RNLI Depot at Poole and sold out of service.

After service
NOTTINGHAMSHIRE was sold out of service in December 1997 to the National Sea Rescue Institute of South Africa for further service as a lifeboat, being renamed Sanlam Rescuer and stationed at Gordon's Bay, near Cape Town, and designated Rescue 9. Unfortunately, Sanlam Rescuer was destroyed in a fire at Bongers Marine, the well-known yacht-building facility owned by Simon Bongers at Gordon's Bay, during a refit in December 2010. She had been withdrawn from service in Gordon's Bay to be refurbished, and was due to be deployed at Mossel Bay.

▲ 33-10 at Oban, July 1994; she served the west coast station for just over eight years. (Nicholas Leach)

▲ 33-10 was sold out of service in 1997 to the NSRI, South Africa, and was renamed Sanlam Rescuer. She served as Gordon's Bay (Rescue 9) lifeboat for thirteen years. (By courtesy of the RNLI)

Safeway (33-11)

Key data

BUILT 1984, Lochin Marine, Rye, Sussex
DONOR Appeal by Safeway Food Stores Ltd
STATIONS Calshot Mar 1985 – Jan 2002
RECORD 259 launches, 40 lives saved
DISPOSAL Sold out of service in June 2002 to NSRI, South Africa without engines

Service history

SAFEWAY was built during 1984 and was completed by Lochin Marine at the end of the year. She was then exhibited at the London International Boat Show in January 1985. She was placed on station at Calshot on 24 March 1985. Provided by the staff and customers of Safeway Food Stores in 1984, she was formally named on 5 July 1985 at Calshot by Mrs Janis Wood, daughter of Safeway's Chairman Terry Spratt, whose wife was meant to name the lifeboat but was unable to do so because of illness. She spent seventeen years on service at Calshot, being taken occasionally to Branksea Marine at Wareham and Berthon Boat Company at Lymington for surveys, maintenance work and hull cleaning. She was replaced at Calshot by Inner Wheel (33-07) and was sold out of service.

After service

SAFEWAY was replaced at Calshot in January 2002 and taken to the RNLI Depot at Poole to be stored and was placed on the sale list. She was sold out of service, without engines, to the NSRI in South Africa and on 19 January 2003 was taken to Sheerness for shipment. She left Sheerness on 28 January 2003 on board a cargo vessel and arrived in South Africa in early February 2003. She was fitted with twin 400hp MTU marine diesel engines driving twin screws through ZF gearboxes, giving a maximum speed of twenty-four knots with a normal operational speed of eighteen to twenty knots depending on conditions. Renamed Eikos Rescuer II, she was placed on station at Durban in 2004, being designated Rescue 5. In May 2019 the boat was replaced by a new ORC 140 type lifeboat, the NSRI's new Class 1 station vessel in place of the Bredes. Eikos Rescuer II was taken out of service and decommissioned in June 2019 and, after sixteen years of NSRI rescue work, was sold to Bosss Marine of Durban in July 2019, and renamed Bosss Charger.

▲ 33-11 on exercise at Calshot in August 1999. (Nicholas Leach)

▲ 33-11 renamed Eikos Rescuer II, designated Rescue 5, on station at Durban

Key data

BUILT 1985, Lochin Marine, Rye, Sussex
DONOR Amateur Swimming Associations of England, Scotland and Wales
STATIONS Relief May 1985 – 1989; Girvan Apr 1989 – Aug 1993
RECORD 48 launches, 20 lives saved (relief); 60 launches, 5 lives saved (Girvan)
DISPOSAL Sold in September 1993 to Nelson Volunteer Coast Guard, New Zealand

Service history

AMATEUR SWIMMING ASSOCIATIONS was built during 1985 and was allocated to the Relief Fleet, completing trials out of the RNLI Depot at Poole in May 1985. She was named on 17 July 1985 at the RNLI Depot, Poole, by Mrs Pat Garforth, wife of the President of the Amateur Swimming Association, which had been raising funds for the RNLI through sponsored swimming events for a number of years. She had already undertaken her first relief duties, at Calshot, by the time of her naming, and throughout the 1980s served at Poole, Alderney, Fowey and Exmouth, as well as Calshot, on temporary duty. In April 1989 she was sent to Girvan to take up station duties in place of Philip Vaux (ON.1084), and spending just over four years at the Ayrshire station.

After service

AMATEUR SWIMMING ASSOCIATIONS was sold out of service in 1993 to the Coastguard at Port Nelson in New Zealand for life-saving work. She was renamed Sealord Rescue, and was based at Nelson, South Island, for eighteen years. Harold Mason, coxswain of the boat in New Zealand, presented a commemorative plaque to the people of Girvan from the residents of Nelson during a visit in 1993. She was sold by the Coastguard in 2012 and bought by a private owner, originally from the Netherlands, who renamed her Girvan and based her at Waikawa Marina in Picton, South Island. She was in

good condition having retained her original twin Caterpillar 3308 engines, but had some minor hull repairs undertaken and was fitted with a toilet and sink. She was relaunched by her new owner in March 2012 as a private pleasure boat (pictured left). In 2020 she was sold again sold and moved to Queen Charlotte Sound, near Picton.

◀ 33-12 at
the RNLI
Depot, Poole,
August 1985.
(Nicholas Leach)

▲ 33-12, renamed Sealord Rescuer, at speed in Tasman Bay, Nelson, New Zealand. (Harold Mason)

Stations served by Bredes

**STATIONS SERVED BY
BREDE LIFEBOATS**

Oban (ON.1080,
   ON.1087, ON.1102)
Fowey (ON.1083)
Girvan (ON.1084 and
   ON.1105)
Exmouth (ON.1088)
Poole (ON.1089)
Alderney (ON.1090)
Invergordon (ON.1102)
Calshot (ON.1089 and
   ON.1104)

**WHAT THE STATIONS
OPERATE IN 2021**

Oban • 14m Trent
Fowey • 14m Trent
Girvan • 13m Shannon
Exmouth • 13m Shannon
Poole • Atlantic 85
Alderney • 14m Trent
Invergordon • 13m
   Shannon
Calshot • Atlantic 85

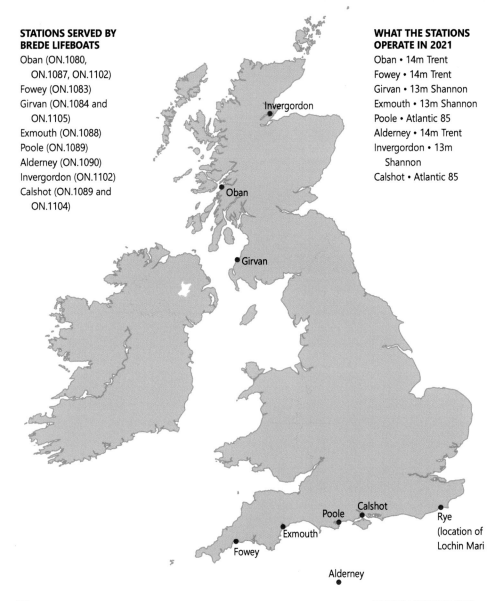